dried flowers

To Doreen
Happy christmas
with love
from Mike + Phic
x

dried flowers

Hilary Mandleberg

designs by
Stephen Woodhams

photography by Simon Brown

Watson-Guptill Publications / New York

First published in Great Britain in 1999
by Ryland Peters & Small,
Cavendish House,
51–55 Mortimer Street,
London W1N 7TD

First published in the United States in 1999 by
Watson-Guptill Publications,
a division of BPI Communications, Inc.,
1515 Broadway, New York, NY 10036

Produced by Sun Fung Offset Binding Co., Ltd
Printed in China

ISBN: 0-8230-2328-1

A CIP catalogue record for this book is
available from the Library of Congress.

First printing, 1999
1 2 3 4 5 6 7 8 9 / 07 06 05 04 03 02 01 99

Publishing Director **Anne Ryland**

Head of Design **Gabriella Le Grazie**

Designer **Sally Powell**

Senior Editor **Hilary Mandleberg**

Editorial Assistant **Maddalena Bastianelli**

Production **Rosanna Dickinson**

Illustrator **Michael Hill**

contents

DRIED FLOWERS HAVE BEEN AROUND FOR AS LONG AS I CAN REMEMBER, but people so often think of them gathering dust in gloomy corners of country cottages that they would not dream of having them in their own homes. It is a challenge to introduce them into contemporary settings, but I hope that this book will prove that it can be done.

If you think about dried flowers at all, you perhaps consider them as something to have in the house in fall or winter, to supplement the limited fresh flowers available at that time of year, or you might be bold enough to think of offering dried red roses to a loved one on Valentine's Day. But to prove to you just how versatile dried flowers can be, I have chosen to take you through the whole year, suggesting ways to use them and showing how appropriate these much-maligned creatures can be, whatever the season.

In this fast-paced age, you may be one of the many who don't have the time or inclination to buy and arrange fresh flowers on a regular basis. If so, a beautiful, long-lasting dried flower arrangement is just the thing to lift your spirits after a long, hectic day. A successful dried-flower arrangement can add the finishing touch to, and strengthen the impact of, any room. It can enhance a color scheme, pick up the mood of the furnishings, complement the textures of fabrics and furniture, or emphasize the scale of a room. And it will easily last four or five years, by which time you will probably be thinking about redecorating anyway.

An arrangement of dried flowers can also serve as a quick and easy table decoration at an impromptu dinner party, or it can make the perfect gift. I nearly always have a small wrapped dried arrangement in the house on standby, in case I'm suddenly invited out to dinner and need to take a present with me. And in case you still need convincing, you should know that recent methods of drying and preserving plants make it possible for

them to retain their beautiful bright colors and textures in a way that was unheard of just a few years ago. Roses and lavender look as fresh as the day they were picked. Preserved foliage could have come straight from the tree. Freeze-dried fruits and vegetables look almost good enough to eat. Even ordinary green carpet moss keeps its color for years.

The optimum atmosphere for keeping dried arrangements at their best is a warm, dry one. Damp conditions will shorten their life, and if the air is too cool, some dried material will start to sweat. And if you need to remove any dust that has settled on your dried arrangement, just waft a hairdryer on a cold setting over it.

Safety is also a consideration where dried material is concerned. If your arrangement is going to stand near an open fire, where sparks might fly, or if it is to include lighted candles, then you should always spray the dried material with a fire-retardant liquid.

And now to the arrangements themselves. In line with current design trends, displays of fresh flowers have moved away from the purely opulent toward cleaner, simpler lines. The same is true of dried flowers, and this is, I think, key to ensuring that dried flower arrangements look right in contemporary settings. What is more, there is now a huge selection of dried tropical material on the market. With their graphic lines, these materials look as if they have been specially grown to suit a minimalist loft apartment or a limestone-lined bathroom. Seashells look great with dried flowers, too, but check with your supplier that the shells have come from countries where efforts are being made to regulate the shell trade, otherwise you could be contributing to the destruction of marine life. This book shows much of this newly available material in use, together with the more traditional material we know and love—peonies, dahlias, marigolds, pinecones, and so on.

I hope you will find much to inspire you within these pages and that these projects will give you the confidence to adapt my designs to suit other material if you wish. I also hope that if, in the past, you decided that dried arrangements were not for you, after reading this book, you will reconsider. Welcome back!

Stephen Woodhams

left and below The wealth of dried material that is available gives me the opportunity for some rather unusual designs. Here I have used bell cups painted duck-egg blue to blend with their blue vase. The spiral positioning of the bell cups complements their lovely shape. This is an arrangement that looks good from any angle.

above The intensity of color of this globe of rich yellow rose heads contrasts glowingly with the muted green freeze-dried moss lining the glass vase. The effect is sublimely springlike.

right Pussy willow is one of the joys of spring. You can buy it ready dried or dry it yourself by simply standing it in a vase without water. It's very important to pick it while it's still at its silvery bud stage, before the stamens emerge.

left Painted red, green, and yellow, these calabash pods remind me of bell peppers, so it seemed natural to put them in a wire basket kitchen container.
below left Yellow and gray is one of my favorite color combinations. Here, I capitalize on it with square galvanized pots filled with yellow rose heads. They add a touch of softness to a modern stainless-steel kitchen.
below right Often a container suggests an arrangement. I couldn't resist the luminous, intense green of this opaque vase. There was no choice but to fill it with dyed green thistles.

spring

It's all been said before, but there's no doubt that spring is when we shed our heavy jackets and look forward to a season of lengthening days, the touch of the sun on our skin, and a fresh new start. It's the same in nature. In the warmth of the sun, bare branches miraculously sprout furry catkins; tight, fat buds unfurl into yellow-green leaves; and dormant lawns suddenly demand their first haircut of the year. As this spring collection goes to show, dried flowers are just as capable of capturing the spirit of the season as fresh ones. Choose from revitalizing greens and yellows or clear sky-blue, and position your designs to make the most of the magical light of spring.

sunny dahlia topiary

Although dahlias are usually thought of as late summer flowers, the sunny open faces of these will brighten up a room in any season. This yellow variety captures the spirit of spring. In a couple of years' time, when the flowers eventually fade, you can create a whole new look with a spray of gold paint.

materials & equipment

pot, 8 inches tall x 7 inches diameter

25–35 birch twigs

2 lengths red-stemmed dogwood, to fit around pot

1 block dry florist's foam, 22 x 13 x 9 inches

10–12 bamboo canes, approximately 18 inches long

1 ball dry florist's foam, 6 inches diameter

dried lichen, to cover

140–160 dried dahlia heads

trimming knife • wire cutters • glue • medium-gauge florist's wire
knife • raffia